PALISADES
MIDDLE SCHOOL
LIBRARY

P9-DDS-819

MACHINES
AND HOW
THEY WORK

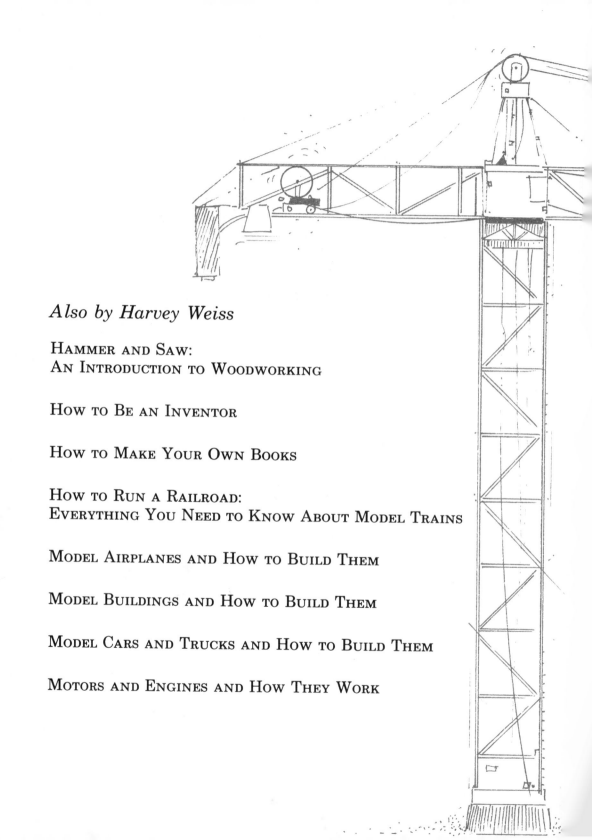

Also by Harvey Weiss

HARVEY WEISS

MACHINES AND HOW THEY WORK

Thomas Y. Crowell   New York

Acknowledgments

The author wishes to thank Bernard M. Jaffe,
professor of physics, Adelphi University,
for his invaluable help in the preparation of
this book.

Machines and How They Work

Copyright © 1983 by Harvey Weiss
All rights reserved. No part of this book may be
used or reproduced in any manner whatsoever without
written permission except in the case of brief quotations
embodied in critical articles and reviews. Printed in
the United States of America. For information address
Thomas Y. Crowell Junior Books, 10 East 53rd Street,
New York, N.Y. 10022.

Library of Congress Cataloging in Publication Data

Weiss, Harvey.
  Machines and how they work.

  Summary: An introduction to six simple
machines—the lever, the inclined plane, the
screw, the wheel and axle, the wedge, and the
pulley—and their use in more complex machines
such as derricks, bulldozers, and metal lathes.
  1. Simple machines—Juvenile literature.
2. Pulleys—Juvenile literature. 3. Gearing—
Juvenile literature. 4. Levers—Juvenile
literature. [1. Simple machines] I. Title.
TJ147.W428 1983   621.8   82-45925
ISBN 0-690-04299-X
ISBN 0-690-04300-7 (lib. bdg.)

Designed by Trish Parcell
10 9 8 7 6 5 4

CONTENTS

INTRODUCTION

Pulleys, wheels and axles, and levers, along with a few other things like the wedge, screw, and inclined plane, are simple machines. Machines make work easier. Machines make holes, chop wood, lift heavy weights, plow fields, and do all sorts of other things that primitive people used to do with slow, backbreaking labor. There are so many different kinds of machines used in the world today that the age we live in is sometimes called the Machine Age.

When we talk about machines, what comes to mind is usually something large and complex, like a derrick or a drilling machine, rather than a crowbar or an ax. But all these things are machines. They are forms of tools that make life much easier for us. The more complicated machines may seem to operate on mysterious and super-sophisticated principles. But you'll find that a good portion of the "insides" of machines like this is really made up of various combinations of simple parts—the sorts of parts and mechanical motions we are concerned with in this book. These basic parts are actually machines themselves. Most physicists agree that there are six. They are:

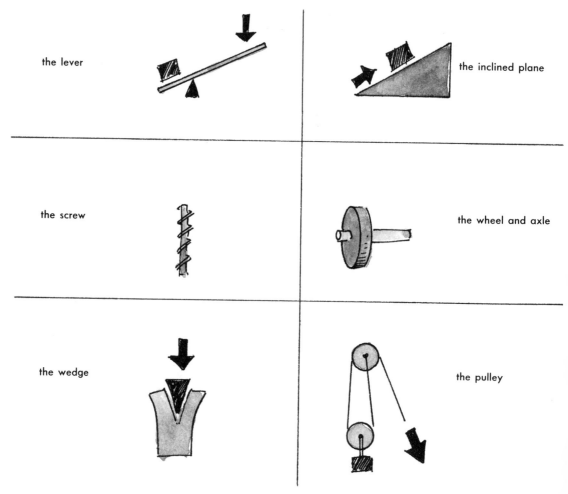

the lever

the inclined plane

the screw

the wheel and axle

the wedge

the pulley

We'll take a look at each one of these simple machines, and then, we'll see how they get used in different ways in all kinds of other machines, from a simple hand saw to a metal lathe or steam engine or diesel-powered bulldozer.

Just about all the machines and mechanical principles that are discussed in this book are very old. Leonardo da Vinci, who lived in Italy in the fifteenth century, left us notebooks full of drawings showing levers, screws, and pulley arrangements similiar to those shown here and on following pages. Scientists like Archimedes (287–212 B.C.) have left us mechanical ideas that are the basis of many modern machines. Archimedes was Greek, but he studied at the university of Alexandria in northern Egypt.

Hundreds of years before the birth of Christ, Alexandria was an important center of learning and discovery. Many scientists, mathematicians, and engineers studied and worked there. One of the most colorful engineers of that time was a man by the name of Hero. Some of his inventions, too, laid the groundwork for present-day technology. The model machine on page 74 is based on an idea of Hero's. If you decide to build this model, you can tell your friends you've built something that was designed about two thousand years ago!

THE LEVER

A lever is one of the simplest mechanical devices. Basically, it is nothing more than a beam or stick or rod of some sort. However, a lever by itself isn't good for much. It must have something on which to pivot. This pivot is called a fulcrum.

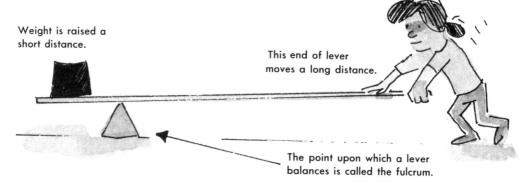

Weight is raised a short distance.

This end of lever moves a long distance.

The point upon which a lever balances is called the fulcrum.

By using a lever, you can move a heavy weight with little effort. But that little effort must be spread over a greater distance than the distance the weight itself is being moved. In other words, you use little effort, but you use it over a longer distance.

easy effort for a
long distance

hard effort for
a short distance

There is a basic principle of physics that describes this business of "hard effort for a short distance" being equal to "easy effort for a long distance." It is called the theory of the conservation of energy. In effect, it says you don't get anything for nothing.

There is a simple formula that is used with levers: The effort multiplied by the distance from the fulcrum equals the weight multiplied by *its* distance from the fulcrum. For example, as shown below, 2 pounds of effort exerted 4 feet from the fulcrum will lift 8 pounds located 1 foot on the other side of the fulcrum.

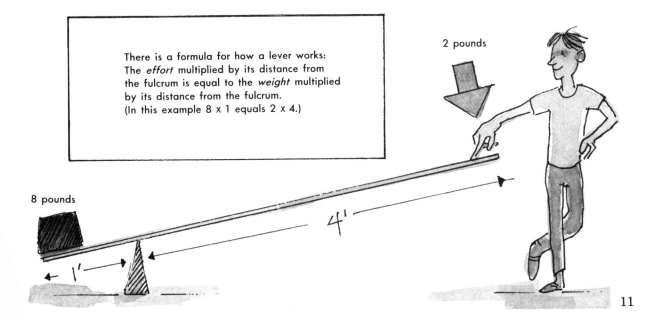

There is a formula for how a lever works: The *effort* multiplied by its distance from the fulcrum is equal to the *weight* multiplied by its distance from the fulcrum.
(In this example 8 x 1 equals 2 x 4.)

2 pounds

8 pounds

4'

1'

There are many possible arrangements of levers. The positions of fulcrum, weight, and effort are different in each case. As we will see, different kinds of levers in many variations are used in all kinds of simple and complex machinery.

In this case the small rock is acting as the fulcrum.

The wheel is the fulcrum here.

In this case the weight is in the center and the lever is being pushed up from the right-hand side.

Here the principle is the same as above, but the effort is now on the left-hand side.

The principle of the lever, as found in the crowbar or seesaw, is quite obvious. But when we get to more complex machines the lever principle is not always so easy to see. In the power shovel, for example, we may not realize that the bucket digging up the dirt is at one end of a large lever.

A few more examples of levers in use are shown here.

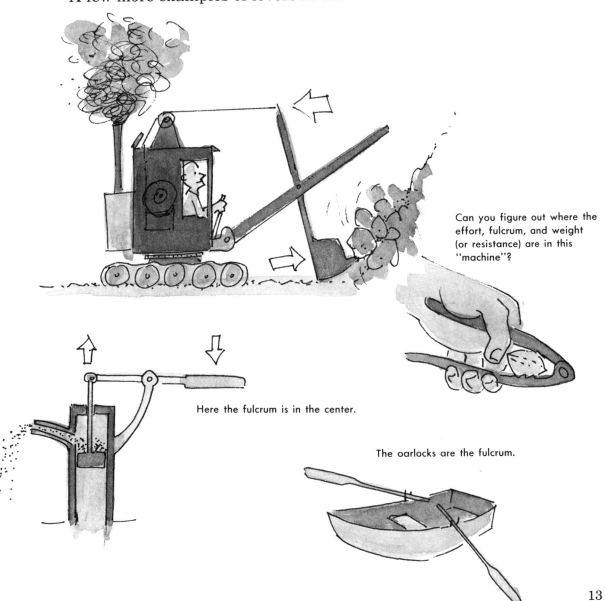

Can you figure out where the effort, fulcrum, and weight (or resistance) are in this "machine"?

Here the fulcrum is in the center.

The oarlocks are the fulcrum.

fulcrum

cylinder

pump

This is a simplified drawing of a very early
steam engine. It was developed by James Watt,
and was used to pump water out of coal mines.
The lever is a massive wood beam that pivots
back and forth. On one side is the steam
cylinder. On the other side is the pump.

14

If you have been to the circus, you have no doubt seen a troupe of tumblers like this. When that fellow jumps off the raised platform and lands on one end of the lever, the person on the other end goes flying through the air.

fulcrum

There are many possible lever arrangements with varied placement of fulcrum, weight, and effort.

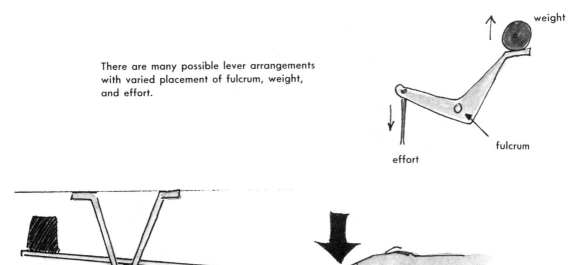

weight

fulcrum

effort

THE INCLINED PLANE

The inclined plane is simply a tilted-up flat surface. It is a ramp. It is a way of raising a load that would otherwise be too heavy to manage.

The angle—that is, the steepness—of the inclined plane determines how much effort is needed to raise the weight. The steeper the ramp, the more effort is required.

In the illustration opposite, you would have to push the box a greater distance when the ramp is at a low angle. With the steeper ramps, you would have to push harder—but for a shorter distance. Though it might not seem that way, both cases would require the same total amount of effort.

An inclined plane may not seem like much of a machine at first. But there are many times when this principle is used. Getting up a mountain is one example. It would take a lot of effort to bicycle straight up the side of a steep mountain. But with an inclined plane—a ramp—you could get to the top with little trouble.

The gorilla isn't using any inclined plane at all, so he must raise or push up the entire weight, getting no mechanical advantage from a ramp.

17

no ramp

ramp

A long ramp going to the top of a mountain might require some difficult and expensive construction. But the same effect can be gotten by making the ramp wind around the side of the mountain. After all, there is no reason why the ramp has to be straight. This is the way most highways and some railroad tracks are constructed when a steep hill or mountain has to be traveled over.

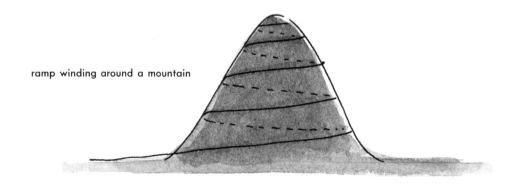

ramp winding around a mountain

Most archaeologists agree that a system of inclined planes was used to build the pyramids.

If we were building a pyramid today, the work would go fast and easy with a few heavy-duty cranes. There wouldn't be any need for the thousands of slaves that the Egyptians used when they built the original pyramids.

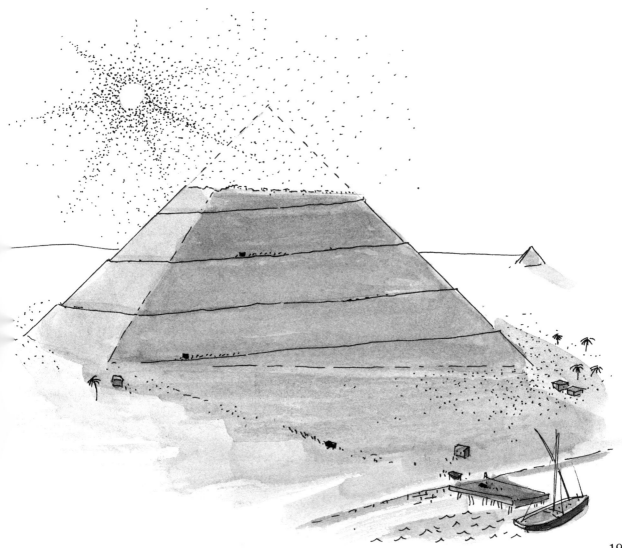

The inclined plane was also used in all likelihood for the erection of various large vertical monuments—everything from totem poles to granite obelisks and ancient statues. The drawings below show some of the steps involved in this kind of operation.

finished statue

On an island in the South Pacific called Easter Island, there are enormous stone statues that scientists believe were carved in the Stone Age. Some of them are over thirty feet tall and weigh many tons. Some had huge head pieces. How were these statues put in place by a primitive people who had few tools? The drawings here show how scientists think it was done, using a system of ramps. After the statue was erected and the head piece put in place, the earth ramps were shoveled away, leaving us with the finished monument.

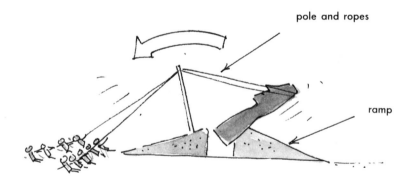

pole and ropes

ramp

head piece

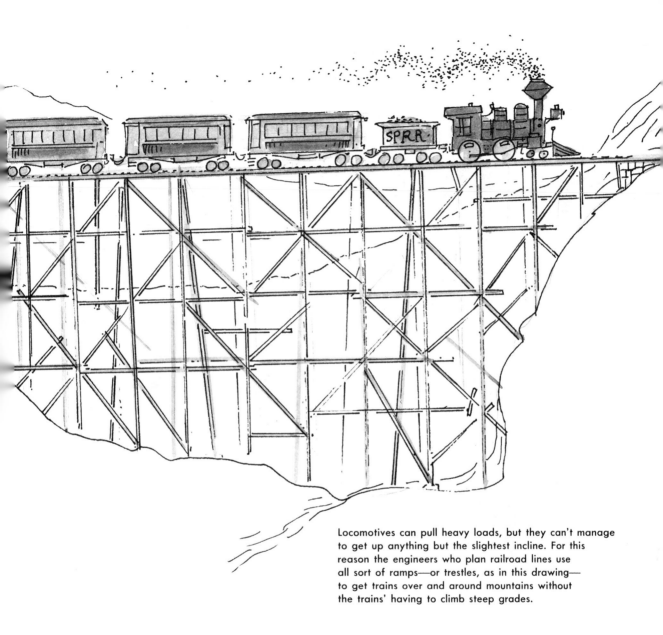

Locomotives can pull heavy loads, but they can't manage
to get up anything but the slightest incline. For this
reason the engineers who plan railroad lines use
all sort of ramps—or trestles, as in this drawing—
to get trains over and around mountains without
the trains' having to climb steep grades.

THE SCREW

The screw is a close relative of the inclined plane. If you take a piece of paper cut to the shape of an inclined plane and wind it around a stick, you will get the form of a screw. It is the same as taking an inclined plane, in the form of a road or railroad tracks, and winding it around a mountain.

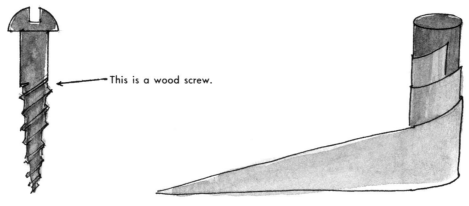

This is a wood screw.

When you twist a wood screw into a piece of wood, you are using one kind of a screw action. The sharp edges of the screw thread are winding their way into the wood and will grip with great strength. This is a very simple kind of screw action.

A different kind of action is used with a nut and bolt. A bolt doesn't have a pointed tip that then gradually widens; it is the same width from one end to the other. The action is one of gripping or holding. Here the screw doesn't create its own track, but must have threading—usually in the form of a nut—that matches the threads of the bolt.

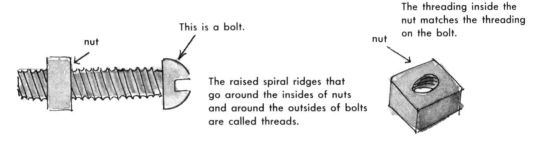

nut

This is a bolt.

The raised spiral ridges that go around the insides of nuts and around the outsides of bolts are called threads.

The threading inside the nut matches the threading on the bolt.

nut

Don't, however, think of the screw as simply a bit of twisted metal used to fasten things together. The "winding" nature of a screw takes many forms. For example, something called a worm gear is used in many machines. The worm gear *worms* along the edge of the larger, round gear. This kind of arrangement is used in many cars to control the position of the front wheels for steering.

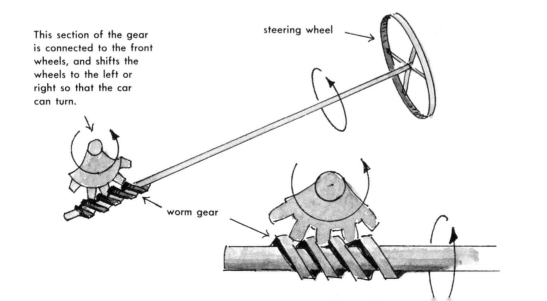

This section of the gear is connected to the front wheels, and shifts the wheels to the left or right so that the car can turn.

steering wheel

worm gear

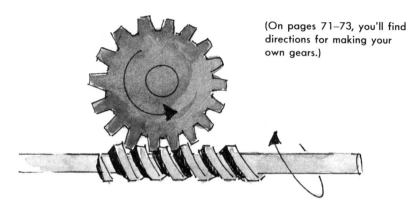

(On pages 71–73, you'll find directions for making your own gears.)

A worm gear is also often used to slow down the speed of rotation of a motor. Even though the worm gear is turning rapidly, the large round gear moves at a much slower rate.

Several different kinds of screw arrangements are shown below and opposite.

As the crank is turned, the screw pulls the two parts of the jack toward one another, causing the top section to rise up.

24

This is a cutaway view of an Archimedian screw. It was invented by Archimedes over two thousand years ago. The screw revolves inside a tube, scooping up water at the bottom and carrying it up and out the top of the tube.

The screw arrangement shown here is used in machines that squeeze down. The first printing press was like this. It squeezed the paper down onto the inked type. (A machine that prints is called a printing *press*.) In a similar way wine presses squeeze down on grapes. As the screw is rotated, the pressure plate descends.

Propellers are a form of screw. The boat propeller twists its way through the water. In fact, old navy salts refer to a ship's propeller as "the screw."

Airplane propellers "screw" their way through the air.

25

THE WEDGE

The wedge is still another variation of the inclined plane. An easy way to see how a wedge works is to think of it as an inclined plane standing on its narrow end. A fairly weak force, applied to the wide end of a wedge whose narrow end is being pushed into something, will produce a strong force pushing out at the sides.

If the wedge is made of steel and banged into the end of a log, the log will split wide open. A knife blade works in pretty much the same way. It is a much sharper and narrower wedge than the log-splitting wedge, but it is doing the same kind of splitting.

The blade of the knife is wedging into the grain of the wood, separating little pieces—chips—from the main body of the wood.

A wedge may seem like the simplest thing in the world. What's so important about splitting logs? But the wedge action is important when you realize that it is also a cutting action. The wedge that splits a log is cutting it into two pieces.

If we use a wedge to cut off small chips of wood, instead of to split up logs, we are doing the kind of cutting that is needed to shape and form all sorts of objects—chair, shelf, totem pole, whatever.

The edge of the knife, or in this case the chisel, is a very narrow wedge.

We can use the wedge action to cut and shape materials such as steel, aluminum, and plastic, too, to make things we need everyday in our lives.

Wood sculpture is produced by cutting away, a chip at a time, until the final form is arrived at.

A cold chisel is used to cut into very hard materials such as steel.

A shovel is acting as a wedge—even if the material is as soft as snow.

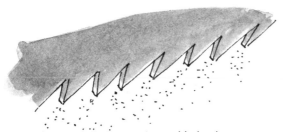

A saw blade also acts as a wedge. The blade is a row of small wedges.

The file, rasp, plane, hatchet—in fact, all tools that cut—are based on the principle of the wedge.

Using the Principle of the Wedge

Power tools that cut

When we begin to use power to do a job of cutting, we find an entirely new family of machines that involve the principle of the wedge. They are called power tools, and they are basic to all kinds of industry.

A lathe is a type of machine that will remove wood—or metal—with great ease and style. It is, in fact, the machinist's favorite tool. In a lathe, the tool doesn't move. The material that is being worked on moves. It rotates. As it turns, the edge of the cutting tool cuts off a small sliver or chip of material. The process of cutting material off a rotating piece of wood or metal is called *turning*. A machinist might say he is "turning down a shaft" to a certain required diameter. The lathe

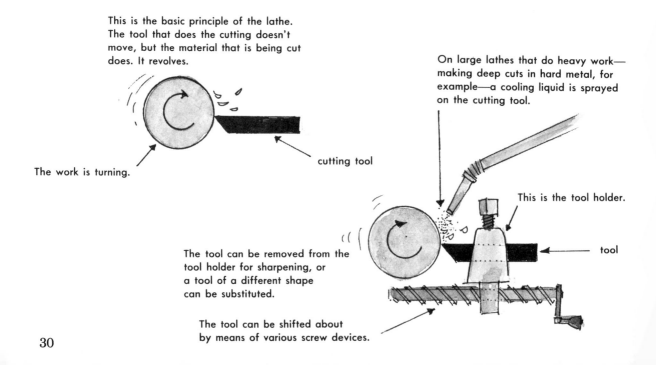

This is the basic principle of the lathe. The tool that does the cutting doesn't move, but the material that is being cut does. It revolves.

The work is turning.

cutting tool

On large lathes that do heavy work—making deep cuts in hard metal, for example—a cooling liquid is sprayed on the cutting tool.

This is the tool holder.

tool

The tool can be removed from the tool holder for sharpening, or a tool of a different shape can be substituted.

The tool can be shifted about by means of various screw devices.

The dotted lines show the material being worked on. The section on the left is powered by a motor and has some means for gripping the work. The device on the right is called the tailstock and holds the tail end of the work. The center part of the lathe is called the carriage. It holds the cutting tool and has various geared mechanisms that enable the tool to move in several different directions.

This section is called the headstock. →

This part holds the work.

the cutting tool

The lathe shown here is the kind used for shaping metal. A woodworking lathe is similar in principle. However, in that kind of lathe a heavy chisel is held by hand against the rotating wood.

All metal lathes have complicated screw arrangements that allow the cutting tool to move in and out and back and forth at various angles.

is not intended to cut large flat or bulky pieces of material. It deals only with circular shapes. Shown below are some examples of power tools used in industry to cut and shape wood and metal.

With a wood lathe, the tool that does the cutting is held by hand. It is a form of chisel. A wood lathe is used to shape things like banisters, chair legs, salad bowls, baseball bats, and all kinds of round objects.

a wood cutting lathe

cutting tool

motor

Shown below are some examples of power tools used in industry to cut and shape wood and metal.

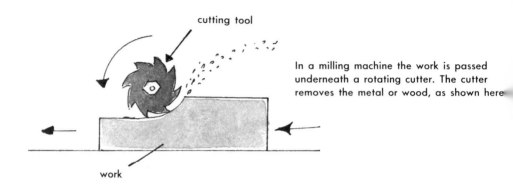

cutting tool

In a milling machine the work is passed underneath a rotating cutter. The cutter removes the metal or wood, as shown here.

work

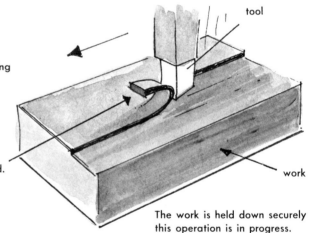

tool

A shaper is a heavy-duty metalworking tool used by machinists. The cutting is done by a blade that moves back and forth across the surface of the metal, shaving off slivers.

Chip or shaving of metal being removed.

work

The work is held down securely this operation is in progress.

When big and complicated tools like these are used in modern industries, they are referred to as machine tools. Some are so large and so complicated, they are controlled by computers and cost hundreds of thousands of dollars. Machine tools include lathes, milling and shaping machines, grinders, polishers, and specialized variations of these in many different sizes for use with wood, plastic, and metal.

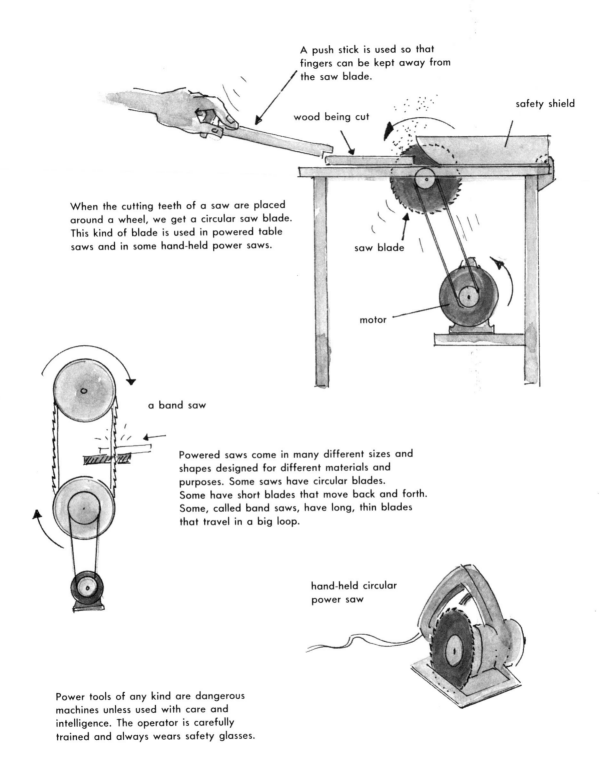

A push stick is used so that fingers can be kept away from the saw blade.

wood being cut

safety shield

saw blade

motor

When the cutting teeth of a saw are placed around a wheel, we get a circular saw blade. This kind of blade is used in powered table saws and in some hand-held power saws.

a band saw

Powered saws come in many different sizes and shapes designed for different materials and purposes. Some saws have circular blades. Some have short blades that move back and forth. Some, called band saws, have long, thin blades that travel in a big loop.

hand-held circular power saw

Power tools of any kind are dangerous machines unless used with care and intelligence. The operator is carefully trained and always wears safety glasses.

a chain saw

The chain saw has a sharp cutting tooth attached to each link of the chain. When the throttle is opened, the chain rotates around a flat steel support. Most chain saws are driven by small gasoline engines, though there are some types that are powered by electric motors.

This is the part that does the cutting.

If we consider a plain old hand shovel a cutting tool—it *does* cut the earth—then we will have to include an entire family of heavy-duty earth-moving equipment that cuts the earth. The bulldozer is the first machine that comes to mind. Even though it is often used as an earth pusher, it does have a sharp blade and is also an earth cutter.

The power shovel is similar, and so are many earth-moving and road-building machines, such as the grader, which scrapes a sharp blade along the surface of the earth.

More Uses of the Wedging Principle
Machines that drill holes

Drilling a hole may not seem much like cutting something with a sharp blade. Yet the process is quite similar. If you look closely at the working end of a drill bit, you will find that it contains two cutting edges. As the drill turns, these edges dig into the material being drilled. It is the same cutting action you get with a knife or with the sort of tool described on the previous several pages.

Although most drill bits work in the same way, the devices that hold them vary—as you can see in the drawings that follow.

cutting edges

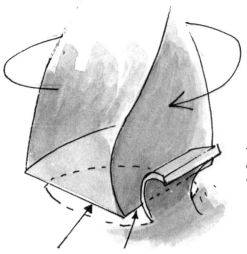

Most people think of a drill as having a rotating point that makes a hole. Actually it is a pair of rotating sharp edges that does the work. And this edge is like the one that carves a piece of wood or splits a log. It is the principle of the wedge at work again, as in all cutting action.

This is a close-up view of the action. The edge of the drill is cutting a chip of wood or metal.

As the drill turns, these sharp edges cut into the material being drilled.

There are many kinds of drills intended for different materials.

This drill uses a hard, sharp edge for cutting through thin materials.

This drill is really a round saw blade. It is used for cutting very large holes in wood.

Some drills are tipped with an extremely hard metal (tungsten carbide) and used for making holes in concrete and stone.

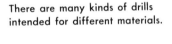

37

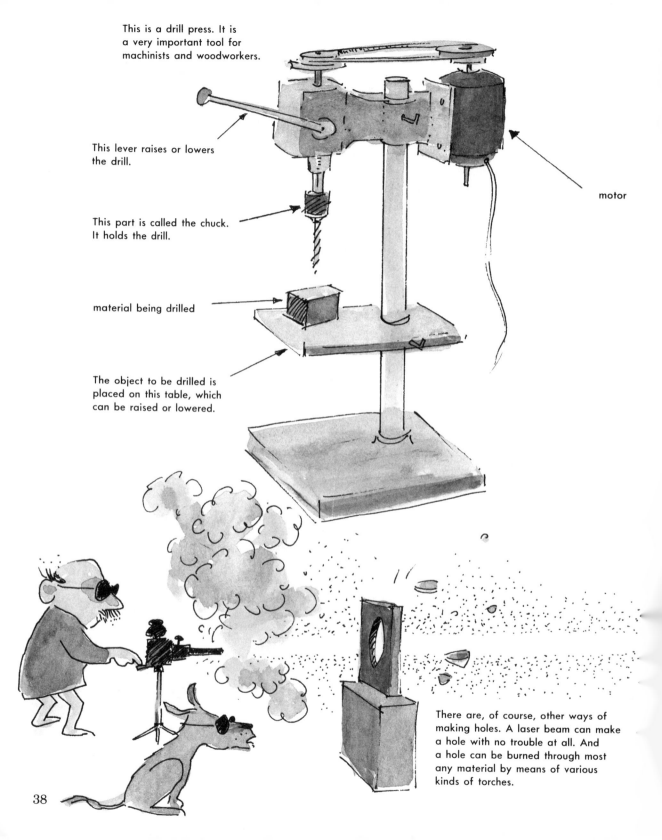

This is a drill press. It is a very important tool for machinists and woodworkers.

This lever raises or lowers the drill.

This part is called the chuck. It holds the drill.

motor

material being drilled

The object to be drilled is placed on this table, which can be raised or lowered.

There are, of course, other ways of making holes. A laser beam can make a hole with no trouble at all. And a hole can be burned through most any material by means of various kinds of torches.

38

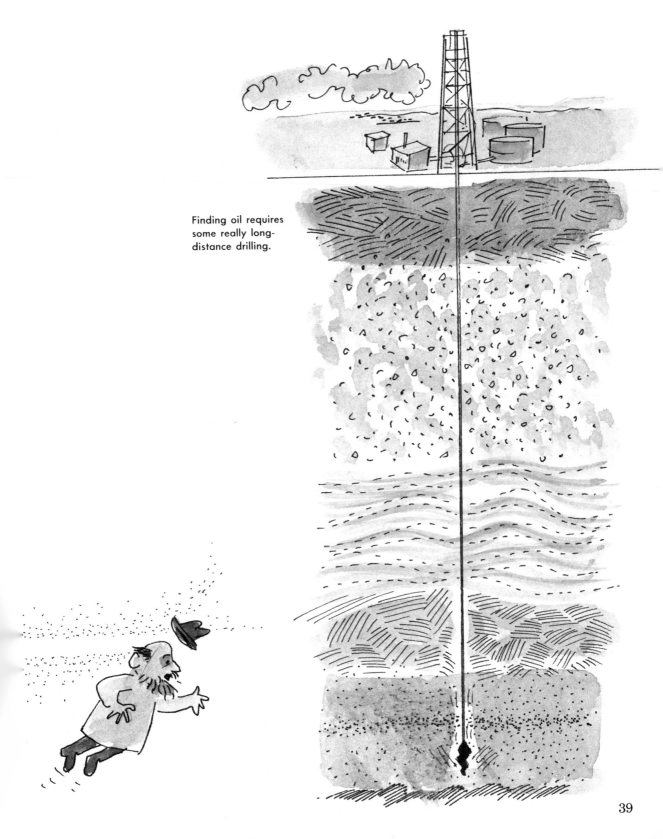

Finding oil requires some really long-distance drilling.

39

THE WHEEL AND AXLE

Civilization would stop dead if the wheel in all its varied forms didn't exist. The wheel is, first of all, important for all kinds of transportation . . . cars, trains, wagons, trucks, and so on. But the wheel has other uses besides moving things around.

The wheel is sometimes called a lever in the round. This may sound very odd at first. How can a lever be a wheel? It becomes clear if you think of a wheel as a series of levers rotating around a centrally placed fulcrum. The axle is, in effect, the fulcrum of the wheel.

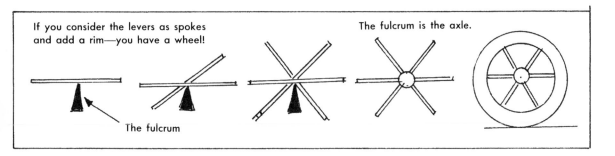

If you consider the levers as spokes and add a rim—you have a wheel!

The fulcrum is the axle.

The fulcrum

The evolution of the lever into the wheel:

This waterwheel is of a type that has been used as a source of power since ancient times. In this case the water comes from above and its weight on the blades of the wheel causes the wheel to turn. The axle would be connected, either directly or by means of gears, to a millstone, a large circular saw blade, or something similar.

When a wheel has spokes coming out of it like this, we get the sort of windlass that old sailing ships used for pulling up their anchors or raising heavy sails.

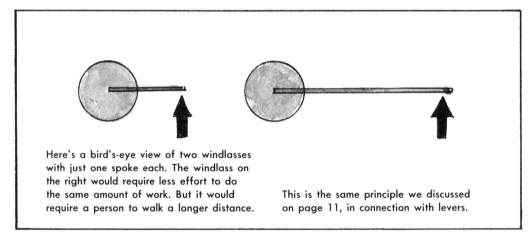

Here's a bird's-eye view of two windlasses with just one spoke each. The windlass on the right would require less effort to do the same amount of work. But it would require a person to walk a longer distance.

This is the same principle we discussed on page 11, in connection with levers.

Ancient monument builders used wooden rollers to transport massive weights. After the weight passed over a roller, the roller was picked up and moved in front of the weight again.

Some wheels serve no purpose other than to reduce friction. Ball bearings are like this. We may consider a ball a kind of wheel without an axle.

Roller bearings are similar to ball bearings. As the name implies, they consist of small rollers instead of balls. In both these types of bearings, friction is reduced because the parts roll along each other rather than sliding or rubbing against each other.

This is what a ball bearing looks like.

People who build machinery try very hard to reduce friction by providing for proper lubrication and by using the right kinds of bearings. Bearings come in all sizes and shapes for all sorts of specialized purposes.

Here is a cross section of a ball bearing.

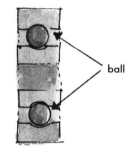

ball

Just about all machines with revolving parts use ball bearings or roller bearings. Cars and trucks have them on their axles and in many places in the engine.

This is a cross section of a roller bearing. As the name implies, short steel rollers are used instead of balls.

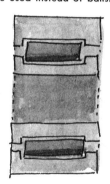

You can think of a roller as a kind of very wide wheel, or as a great many wheels placed side by side. The purpose of a roller is to reduce friction. It is much easier to roll something along than to drag or carry it.

A flywheel is any large heavy wheel that will smooth out an interrupted power thrust. Take a one-cylinder gasoline engine, for example. Every time the cylinder fires, the crankshaft is given a push. Suppose the crankshaft is given a push down. How does it get back up again? How does the piston get back up to the top of the cylinder ready for the next push? It can get back up only if the crankshaft is attached to a heavy flywheel which has enough momentum to keep turning after being given a push. In large engines with many cylinders, there are closely spaced power thrusts, so a smooth motion is obtained and a large flywheel is not needed.

A flywheel makes use of the principle of inertia. Inertia is defined as the tendency of an object to remain at rest if it is already at rest—or to remain in motion if it is already in motion. Another way of saying it is that inertia is the tendency of an object to continue doing what it is already doing. The larger and heavier a flywheel, the more inertia it will have.

In all machines where there are moving parts, a certain amount of energy is lost due to friction. In large machines with many parts, this loss of energy means a lot of waste and a serious buildup of heat. For this reason provisions for oiling and the use of bearings are designed into most machines. (If an automobile engine ran with no oil, the heat from friction would ruin it in only a few minutes.)

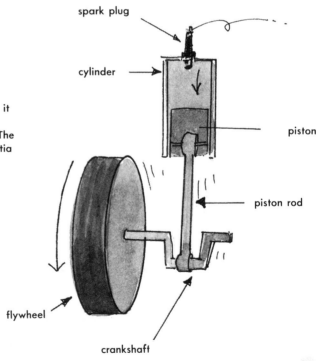

spark plug

cylinder

piston

piston rod

flywheel

crankshaft

A potter's wheel is another kind of flywheel. The potter kicks the wheel to keep it turning. The wheel is a massive iron or concrete affair, so when it has been kicked a few times and is revolving steadily, it will keep going for quite some time.

If the wheel is laid down flat and arranged as shown here, you get a potter's wheel. The bottom wheel is heavy, and is kept turning by kicks from the potter's foot. The smaller, upper wheel holds the clay.

How about a wheel that has its axle off-center? A wheel like this would give a terribly bumpy ride if used on a car or truck. But it does have a practical use in many machines. An off-center wheel, or a wheel with a "bump" on it, is called a *cam*. It serves to move a lever at a predetermined interval.

A cam of one sort or another is used in most gasoline engines to open and shut the valves. The valves have to operate at the proper time to let an explosive gas-air mixture into the cylinders. Another set of cams operates the valves that let the gases out of the cylinder after they have been burned.

Sometimes an oval wheel is used, instead of a round wheel that is off-center.

This rod moves up and down as the cam revolves.

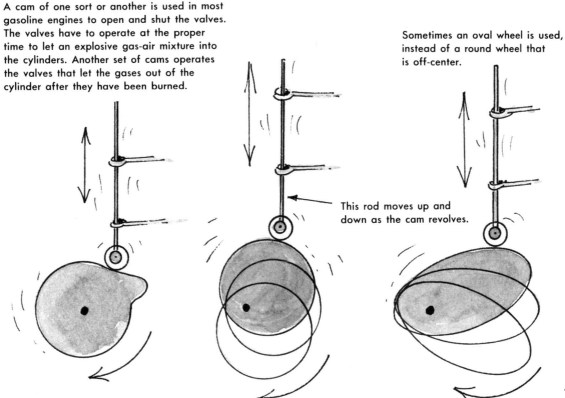

45

Gears: *Wheels with teeth*

A gear is a wheel with teeth along the outer edge. By itself a gear can't do much of anything. But in combination with other gears a lot of things can happen. Gears can transfer effort from one place to another. Gears can change the speed of rotation. Gears can change the direction of rotation. And gears can change the form of mechanical motion.

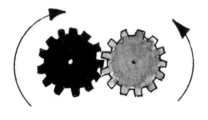

One gear will turn in one direction and the other gear in the opposite direction.

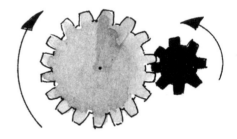

The large gear on the left will turn much more slowly than the smaller gear on the right.

Gears come in many shapes and forms.

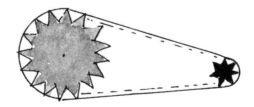

A sprocket gear is one that has teeth designed to work with a chain. A bicycle has sprocket gears.

Here is a worm gear connected to a straight gear.

These are called bevel gears.

If you have a bike that can shift gears, you may already know a great deal about this matter. If you are going fast on a level or downhill stretch, your feet are turning a large gear, which is making a small gear (connected to the rear wheel) turn much faster. When you are going

As you went downhill, your feet would be turning the pedal gear slowly, but the gear on the back wheel would be turning very fast.

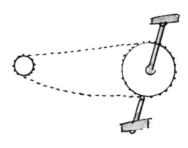

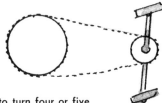

As you went uphill, your feet would be turning the small gear very fast to give the large gear on the back wheel as much power as possible.

The small gear may have to turn four or five times for a single turn of the large gear.

up a hill, you shift gears so your feet are turning a small gear at a fast rate, and this is connected to a larger gear that is turning more slowly. The principle of the lever applies: You use less effort but apply it over a greater distance—the longer circumference of the larger gear.

This combination of gears is called a rack and pinion. The rack (the straight part) moves back and forth as the round gear revolves.

This is a ratchet gear. The teeth are slanted to the right.

pawl

The ratchet gear can turn only to the left. The pawl drops down behind each tooth in turn as the gear revolves. This prevents the gear from turning to the right.

The simplest kind of gear is called a spur gear.

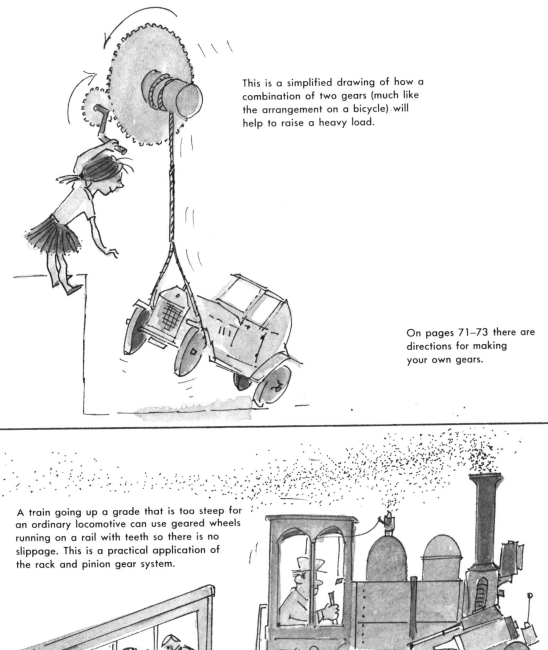

This is a simplified drawing of how a combination of two gears (much like the arrangement on a bicycle) will help to raise a heavy load.

On pages 71–73 there are directions for making your own gears.

A train going up a grade that is too steep for an ordinary locomotive can use geared wheels running on a rail with teeth so there is no slippage. This is a practical application of the rack and pinion gear system.

THE PULLEY

A pulley is nothing more than a grooved wheel that turns on an axle. The groove in the wheel is there so that a rope or cable will ride on the wheel without slipping off. The pulley can do many things.

1. It can change the direction of a pull. In this case, pulling down on the rope will lift the weight up. With just the one pulley there is no saving of effort. It is simply a way to maneuver the weight a little more conveniently. In the example shown below, the job of getting hay up into the barn, it is easier to pull the rope down than to stand up on the barn loft and pull the rope up.

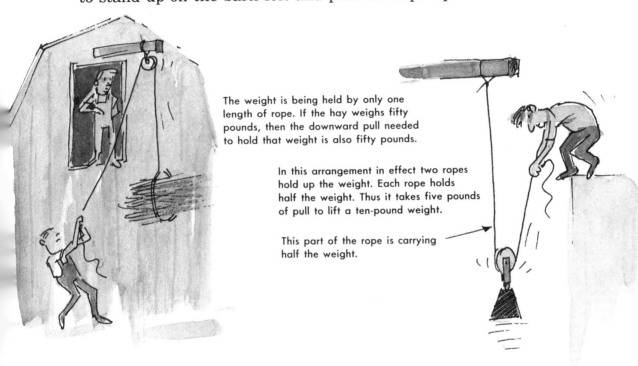

The weight is being held by only one length of rope. If the hay weighs fifty pounds, then the downward pull needed to hold that weight is also fifty pounds.

In this arrangement in effect two ropes hold up the weight. Each rope holds half the weight. Thus it takes five pounds of pull to lift a ten-pound weight.

This part of the rope is carrying half the weight.

2. With the arrangement shown above, right, less effort is required. Half the weight is supported by the overhead beam, and half is supported by the person holding the other end of the rope. The weight is shared. However, now the rope will have to be pulled twice the distance. You would have to use half as much force for *twice* the distance, as in the first example shown above.

When several pulleys are combined, the assembly is called a block and tackle. All derricks and cranes make use of some sort of block-and-tackle arrangement. Even the biggest diesel engines are not powerful enough to lift huge steel girders or heavy buckets of cement without the help of pulleys.

The Greek scientist Archimedes combined several pulleys so that heavy weights could be lifted without too much effort.

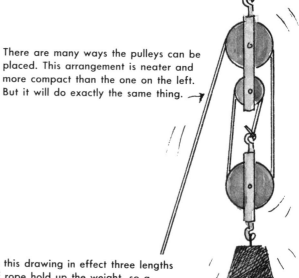

There are many ways the pulleys can be placed. This arrangement is neater and more compact than the one on the left. But it will do exactly the same thing. →

In this drawing in effect three lengths of rope hold up the weight, so a ten-pound pull will lift a thirty-pound weight. However, you would have to pull the rope three times as far.

To raise and control the sails on a boat, you need a variety of pulleys.

There are many ways in which pulleys can be used. On a sailboat, the sail is raised on the mast by a simple pulley arrangement. And a somewhat more complex arrangement of pulleys is used to control the position of the boom to which the bottom of the mainsail is attached.

In an old grandfather clock—where the power source is a heavy weight rather than springs or an electric motor—a block and tackle keeps the weight from sinking down too rapidly.

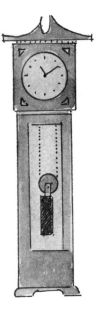

MACHINES IN COMBINATION

Some simple machines are used by themselves—like a crowbar or chisel or loading ramp on a truck. In other cases, these basic machine principles work hand in hand with one another. A lever might be actuated by a system of gears, for example. Or a system of ball bearings might help a cutting tool move along the surface of a steel bar. And, of course, large and complex machines like derricks and bulldozers may contain hundreds of small machine parts working together in carefully designed harmony to accomplish a specific task.

Some of the less complicated machine combinations are shown here.

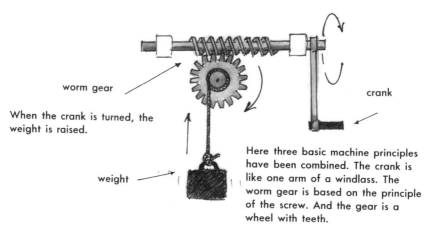

worm gear

crank

When the crank is turned, the weight is raised.

weight

Here three basic machine principles have been combined. The crank is like one arm of a windlass. The worm gear is based on the principle of the screw. And the gear is a wheel with teeth.

pulley

hammer

This is a simple form of trip-hammer. The projections on the wheel push the hammer handle down, then release it as the wheel turns. When the next projection touches the handle, the cycle starts all over again. Huge machines based on this principle are used to pound red-hot steel or iron into shape.

motor

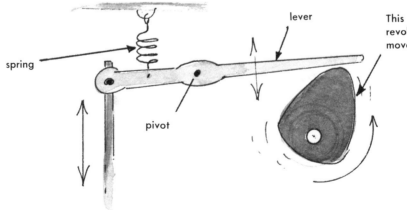

spring

pivot

lever

This off-center wheel (or cam) is revolving and making the lever move up and down.

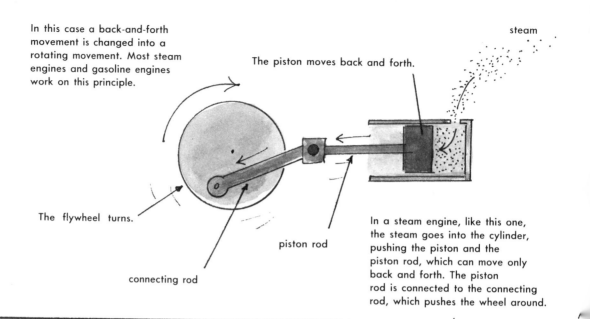

In this case a back-and-forth movement is changed into a rotating movement. Most steam engines and gasoline engines work on this principle.

The piston moves back and forth.

steam

The flywheel turns.

connecting rod

piston rod

In a steam engine, like this one, the steam goes into the cylinder, pushing the piston and the piston rod, which can move only back and forth. The piston rod is connected to the connecting rod, which pushes the wheel around.

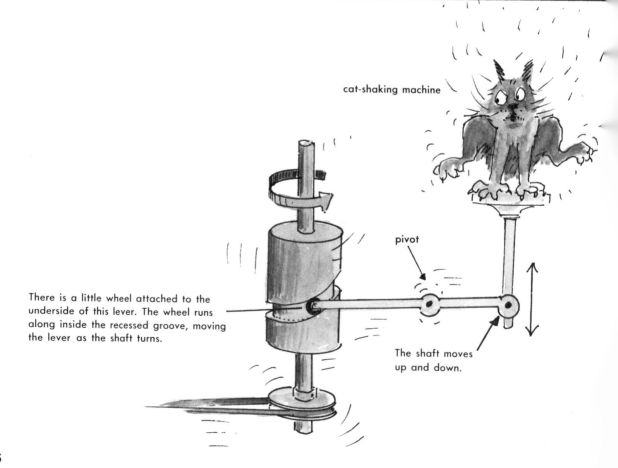

cat-shaking machine

pivot

There is a little wheel attached to the underside of this lever. The wheel runs along inside the recessed groove, moving the lever as the shaft turns.

The shaft moves up and down.

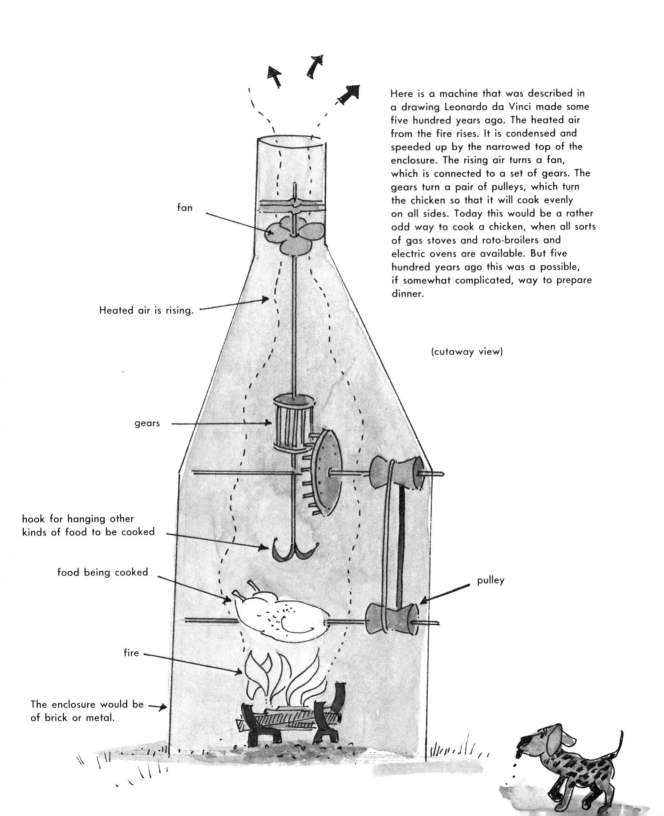

fan

Heated air is rising.

Here is a machine that was described in a drawing Leonardo da Vinci made some five hundred years ago. The heated air from the fire rises. It is condensed and speeded up by the narrowed top of the enclosure. The rising air turns a fan, which is connected to a set of gears. The gears turn a pair of pulleys, which turn the chicken so that it will cook evenly on all sides. Today this would be a rather odd way to cook a chicken, when all sorts of gas stoves and roto-broilers and electric ovens are available. But five hundred years ago this was a possible, if somewhat complicated, way to prepare dinner.

(cutaway view)

gears

hook for hanging other kinds of food to be cooked

food being cooked

pulley

fire

The enclosure would be of brick or metal.

PRIME MOVERS—
WHAT MAKES IT GO

The prime mover is what makes a machine run. The simplest form of prime mover is human muscle power. When you use your strong back and arm muscles to shovel dirt or snow, you are being a prime mover! And the machine is the shovel.

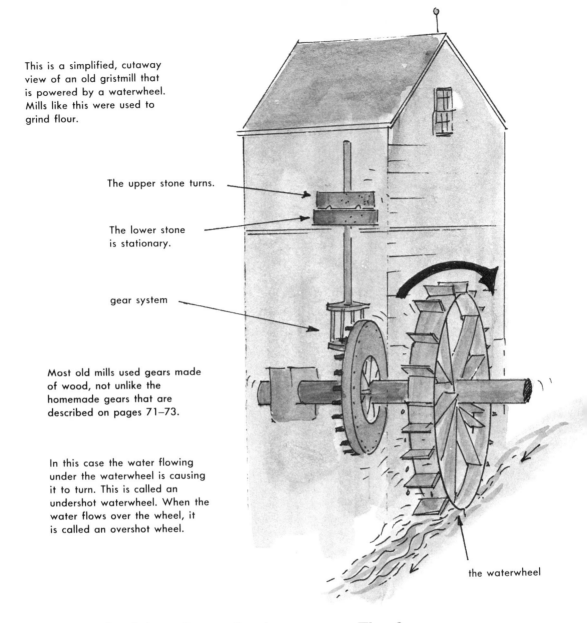

This is a simplified, cutaway view of an old gristmill that is powered by a waterwheel. Mills like this were used to grind flour.

The upper stone turns.

The lower stone is stationary.

gear system

Most old mills used gears made of wood, not unlike the homemade gears that are described on pages 71–73.

In this case the water flowing under the waterwheel is causing it to turn. This is called an undershot waterwheel. When the water flows over the wheel, it is called an overshot wheel.

the waterwheel

A waterwheel is a form of prime mover. The force of the running water makes the wheel turn, and the wheel can be geared to all kinds of machines. Waterwheels were once used to power all sorts of mills—from cutting lumber to grinding corn. Some of the more common prime movers are listed here.

The wind is the energy source for windmills. There are many places all over the world—hill tops, open plains, lake and ocean sites—where the wind is blowing practically all the time.

Scientists are experimenting with modern propeller designs and special electric generating machines. These new windmills, when perfected, will be able to produce cheap and plentiful electricity.

You might say that the energy making the windmill turn is coming from the sun. The sun is heating the surface of the earth, causing the air to rise, and this rising air produces wind currents.

Windmills don't need gale winds in order to do their job. Most will begin to turn if there is wind as slow as five miles an hour. If there is too much wind, a modern windmill will stop automatically in order to prevent runaway speed and damage to the blades, gears, and generator.

A heavy-duty earth scraper such as this needs a rugged, hardworking diesel engine.

Gasoline and diesel engines are the prime movers for all kinds of vehicles, as well as many large-scale machines—everything from model airplanes to ocean liners and giant earthmovers.

No, this is not what is meant by a dogsled.

In early times, animal power was the most common prime mover. Everything from elephants to bulls, donkeys, and dogs was used. The prime mover for a dogsled was none other than . . . That's right!

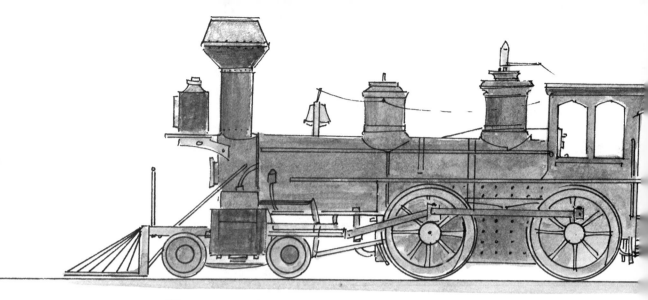

Years ago, the steam engine was one of the most efficient and common prime movers. The usual fuels were coal, wood, or oil. The steam locomotive is just a mobile form of steam engine.

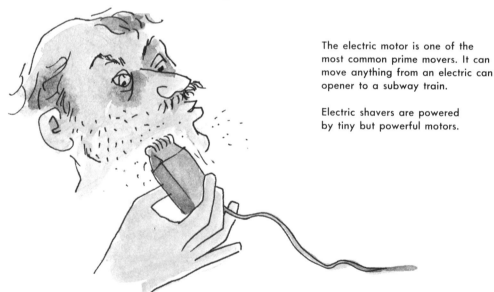

The electric motor is one of the most common prime movers. It can move anything from an electric can opener to a subway train.

Electric shavers are powered by tiny but powerful motors.

The electric motor is particularly useful, because it is available in just about any size, from tiny fractional horsepower size to mammoth locomotive motors.

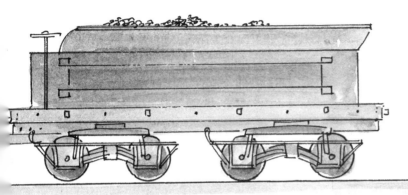

This type of coal-burning locomotive was a common sight during the 1850's. Nowadays most locomotives are diesel or electric.

The prime movers mentioned here make the machines work. But what makes the prime movers work? They need some kind of fuel. This can be anything from the explosive energy of gasoline to the heat from burning coal. It can be steam produced by water boiling in an atomic generator. For humans and animals, it is the food they eat.

These energy sources that fuel the prime movers come from the basic source of all energy—the sun. It is sun that causes the food to grow that human and animal prime movers consume. It is the sun that provides the wind and running water and the plant life that produce coal and wood and oil. But energy and its uses in various forms is a complex subject and beyond the scope of this book.

SIMPLE MACHINES YOU CAN BUILD

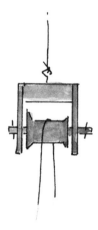

If you want to experiment with the principle of the pulley, you can make a lightweight block and tackle yourself with just a few simple parts. You might find it handy for lifting packages to upstairs windows, or you might want to make some realistic operating derricks for use on a model railroad.

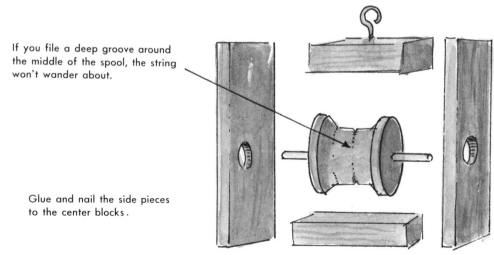

If you file a deep groove around the middle of the spool, the string won't wander about.

Glue and nail the side pieces to the center blocks.

The sort of block and tackle shown here is only for experimenting and lifting light weights. If you want to do some really heavy lifting, you will have to use a much more rugged type of construction.

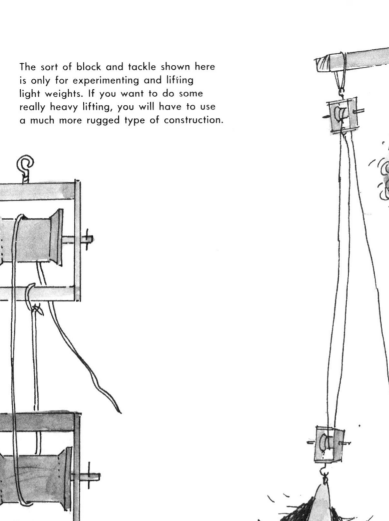

Shown below is a simple but fascinating and useful machine called a Chinese windlass. It consists of two drums of slightly different diameters. A rope goes around one drum, through a pulley, and onto the other drum. A very slight turning effort on the crank handle will lift a heavy weight.

The difference between the diameters of the two drums determines how much effort is needed. If the two drums were the same size no effort at all would be required, but no work would be done—that is, the weight would not be lifted.

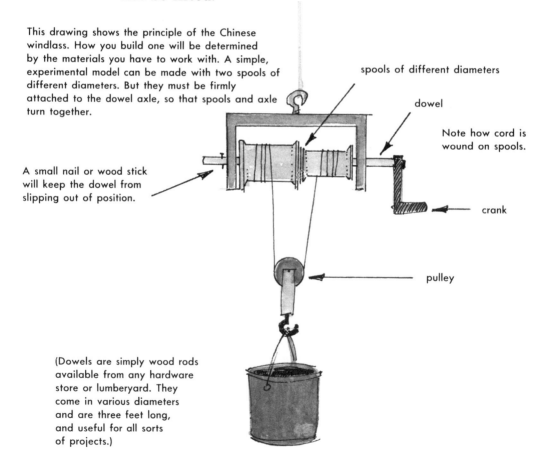

This drawing shows the principle of the Chinese windlass. How you build one will be determined by the materials you have to work with. A simple, experimental model can be made with two spools of different diameters. But they must be firmly attached to the dowel axle, so that spools and axle turn together.

spools of different diameters

dowel

Note how cord is wound on spools.

A small nail or wood stick will keep the dowel from slipping out of position.

crank

pulley

(Dowels are simply wood rods available from any hardware store or lumberyard. They come in various diameters and are three feet long, and useful for all sorts of projects.)

A simple, hand-operated lathe is another machine that isn't too difficult to make. This sort of lathe is still used in some very primitive societies. It's not a machine you can use to make a crankshaft for a small engine. But you can make some candlesticks or decorative turnings, and it will give you a very clear idea of just how a lathe works.

This kind of lathe is called a bow lathe. A bow is used to turn the work. The work turns in one direction; then, at the end of the stroke, it reverses.

The bow lathe was used for thousands of years by primitive craftsmen. However, it is suitable only for light work because one hand must be working the bow, and that leaves only one hand to hold the tool.

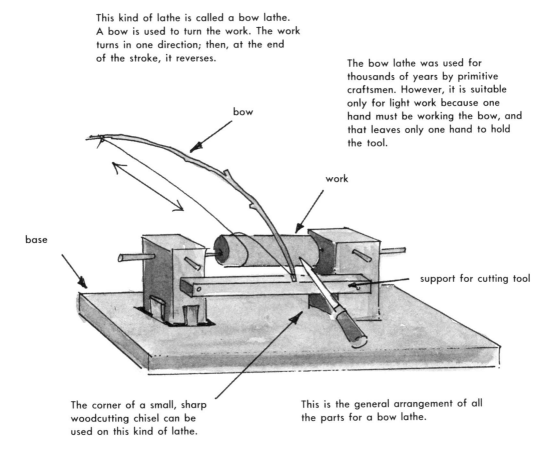

bow

work

base

support for cutting tool

The corner of a small, sharp woodcutting chisel can be used on this kind of lathe.

This is the general arrangement of all the parts for a bow lathe.

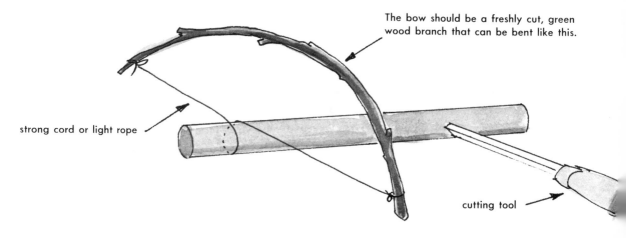

The bow should be a freshly cut, green wood branch that can be bent like this.

strong cord or light rope

cutting tool

Making the bow is easy. The tricky part is making a support for the work that allows it to turn freely and yet will withstand the pressure of the cutting tool. A number of possible arrangements are shown here.

This method of supporting the ends of the work requires an angle iron and some screws and nuts and bolts.

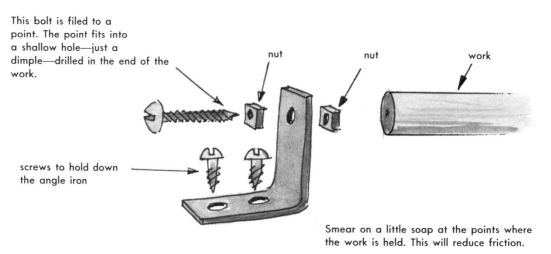

This bolt is filed to a point. The point fits into a shallow hole—just a dimple—drilled in the end of the work.

nut

nut

work

screws to hold down the angle iron

Smear on a little soap at the points where the work is held. This will reduce friction.

This arrangement is used at both ends of the lathe.

Here is an old-fashioned but effective way to hold a piece of wood in place in a lathe while it is being shaped. Two holes are drilled all the way through a block of wood. The upper hole is positioned so that it cuts through the upper part of the lower hole. This is how it works: The work-holding dowel with the pointed end is slid through its hole and into the dimple in the end of the work. In order to keep this dowel from shifting about, another tapered dowel is tapped into place in the other hole. Because the two holes intersect, the tapered dowel will jam up against the work-holding dowel, holding it securely.

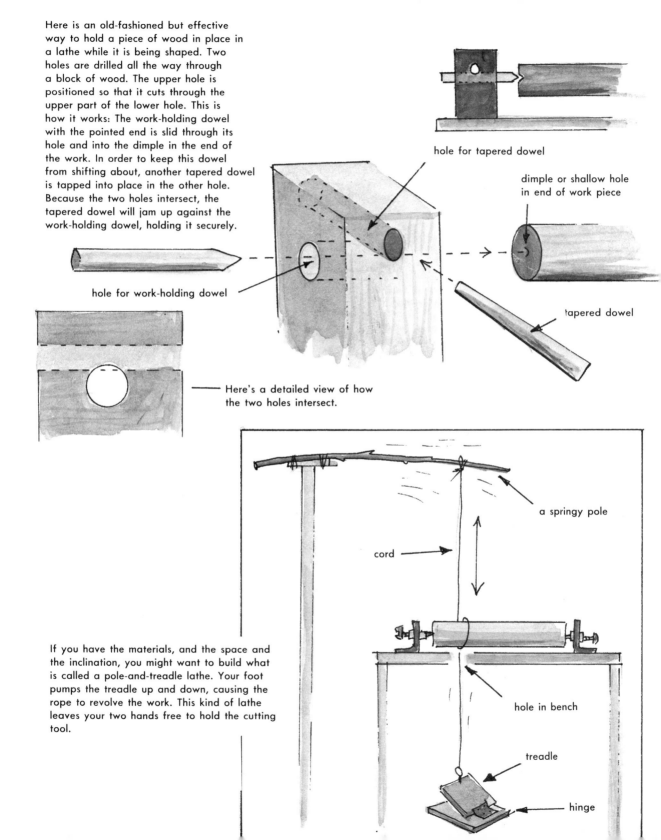

hole for tapered dowel

dimple or shallow hole in end of work piece

hole for work-holding dowel

tapered dowel

Here's a detailed view of how the two holes intersect.

a springy pole

cord

hole in bench

treadle

hinge

If you have the materials, and the space and the inclination, you might want to build what is called a pole-and-treadle lathe. Your foot pumps the treadle up and down, causing the rope to revolve the work. This kind of lathe leaves your two hands free to hold the cutting tool.

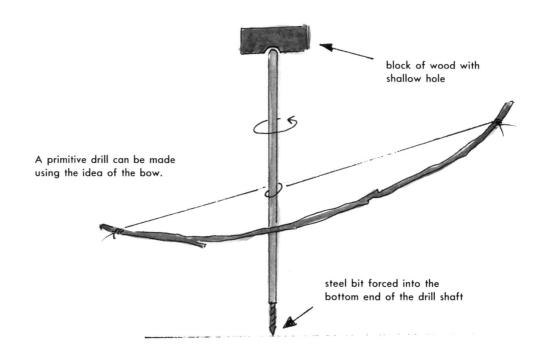

A primitive drill can be made using the idea of the bow.

block of wood with shallow hole

steel bit forced into the bottom end of the drill shaft

Prehistoric people used a similar machine to make a fire. The friction of the stick rotating against a piece of wood made enough heat to start some dry grass smoldering. And this could be built up into a fire.

You can make your own gears if you are careful, neat, and patient. If you try to do this job in a rush, you will end up with something sloppy and disappointing that won't work well.

You may want to make a set of gears just to see how they look and work, or you may have some practical purpose in mind. Perhaps there is a small stream near where you live, and you want to rig up a little water wheel to turn a grindstone for sharpening knives. Maybe you want to build a windmill.

compass

The placement of the teeth in any kind of gear is extremely important. They must all be of the same size and evenly spaced. First make a careful drawing on paper. Then transfer the design by tracing it onto the wood, or by using pinpricks.

Here's a simple method for locating the position of the teeth on a gear. Start with an accurate square drawn on paper. Draw lines from corner to corner to find the center. With a compass draw a circle the size the gear is to be. Draw lines perpendicular to the sides of the square to divide the circle into eighths.

You can divide into smaller segments by making arcs from point A and point B as shown. Then draw a line from where the arcs intersect to the center of the circle. Continue around the circle. You can repeat this method to get additional teeth even closer together.

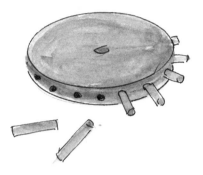

After you have worked out the location of the teeth and transferred their positions to the wood, drill the holes for the dowels. The size of the dowels you use will depend on how large you want your gears to be.

Use a dab of glue to hold the dowels in place.

A ¼-inch dowel is suitable for most gears. (Of course, a ¼-inch hole must be drilled for a ¼-inch dowel.)

When you make this kind of gear, fasten the two pieces of wood together when you drill the holes. This will ensure that the gear teeth line up.

The dowels can be placed on the face of the gear, or they can be placed on the edge if the wood is thick enough.

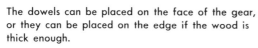
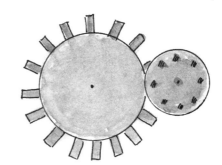

Depending on what you are trying to accomplish, there are many different ways to arrange the gears.

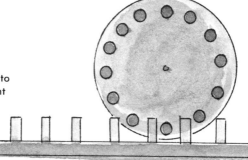

You might want to try making gears with cutout teeth like this. Thin, hard wood is needed for this, and it is a very tricky business indeed. You need good tools, and lots of patience. It is much easier to make gears using dowel pegs set into wood disks. The peg method was used in many old mills, and is shown in some of Leonardo da Vinci's drawings.

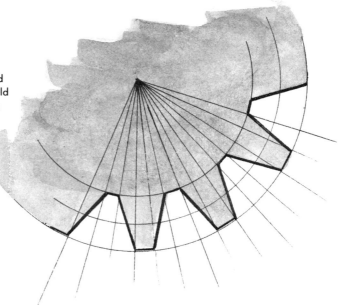

This little machine will amaze and dumbfound anybody you show it to. Put it down on a flat surface, wait a moment or two, and it will begin to slowly roll along. It will inch along for two or three feet, stop for a bit, then slowly roll back to where it started from. The power (the prime mover) is a heavy lead weight that slowly descends. There is a thin string that runs over pulleys and is wrapped around the front axle. The rate at which the lead weight drops is controlled by the sand on which it is resting. The sand runs through a hole in the upper

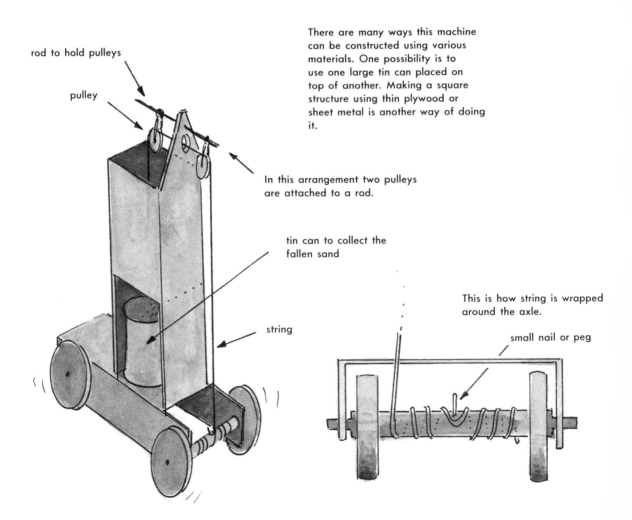

rod to hold pulleys

pulley

There are many ways this machine can be constructed using various materials. One possibility is to use one large tin can placed on top of another. Making a square structure using thin plywood or sheet metal is another way of doing it.

In this arrangement two pulleys are attached to a rod.

tin can to collect the fallen sand

string

This is how string is wrapped around the axle.

small nail or peg

compartment—like an hourglass. As the sand runs out, the weight drops, causing the wheels to turn.

The direction of motion of the little wagon changes because of the way the string is wrapped around the axle. It is wound in one direction for five or six turns. Then a little loop is made, and another five or six turns are wound around the axle in the opposite direction.

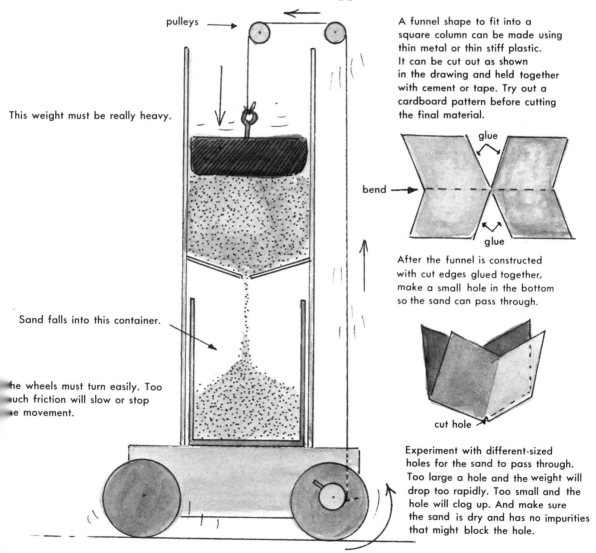

pulleys

A funnel shape to fit into a square column can be made using thin metal or thin stiff plastic. It can be cut out as shown in the drawing and held together with cement or tape. Try out a cardboard pattern before cutting the final material.

glue

bend

glue

This weight must be really heavy.

After the funnel is constructed with cut edges glued together, make a small hole in the bottom so the sand can pass through.

Sand falls into this container.

he wheels must turn easily. Too uch friction will slow or stop e movement.

cut hole

Experiment with different-sized holes for the sand to pass through. Too large a hole and the weight will drop too rapidly. Too small and the hole will clog up. And make sure the sand is dry and has no impurities that might block the hole.

A derrick like the one shown here can be built as a toy for a young friend, or it can be built on a small scale as part of a model railroad landscape, or still another possibility is to build it very neatly and carefully as a working machine that uses some of the mechanical operations this book has discussed. Good material, careful, unrushed workmanship, and a slick paint job will produce a handsome model worth prominent display space.

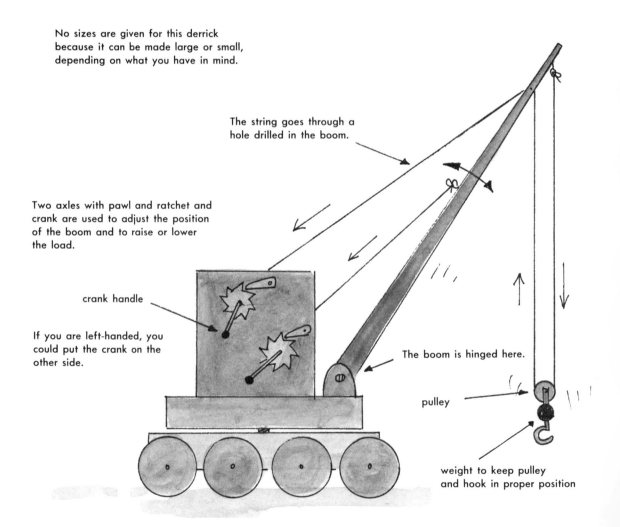

No sizes are given for this derrick because it can be made large or small, depending on what you have in mind.

The string goes through a hole drilled in the boom.

Two axles with pawl and ratchet and crank are used to adjust the position of the boom and to raise or lower the load.

crank handle

If you are left-handed, you could put the crank on the other side.

The boom is hinged here.

pulley

weight to keep pulley and hook in proper position

pawl held in place with nut and bolt

In order to lower the boom
or the pulley, the pawls
must be raised.

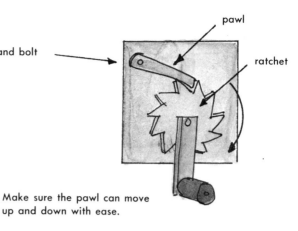

A rachet and pawl (see page 48) can
be added to any windup device
without too much trouble. This kind
of gear is particularly useful on
model derricks, where you don't
want the load to drop down if you
take your hand off the crank.

Make sure the pawl can move
up and down with ease.

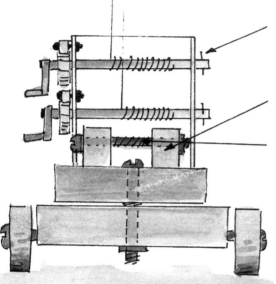

Use a small nail or wrapping of
thread to keep the dowel from
slipping out of position.

The boom, which is not shown
for purposes of clarity,
fits between these two
blocks of wood.

bolt that holds the boom

The upper part of the derrick
can be made to turn if it is
held loosely in place by a
nut and bolt.

front view

You might want to get fancy and try
a bucket arrangement like this. See
if you can figure out how to run a
third control line that will open or
close the back end of the bucket.

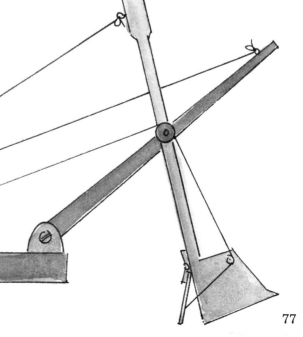

FURTHER READINGS

The mechanical principles described in this book, and their applications in various machines, are part of the science of physics. There are many other aspects to this science—electricity, liquids, sound, optics, and heat, to name a few.

Your school or public library will have a wide variety of books on physics at varying levels of complexity. If you want to read further about some of the specific subjects mentioned in this book, look for more technical books about machines in general or machines for metal- and woodworking. You might also want to read about some of the inventors who developed the machines we use today: Archimedes, Hero, Robert Fulton, Thomas Edison, James Watt, Leonardo da Vinci . . . You can, of course, look for a very particular subject that interests you. For example, see what you can find on the radio or magnetism, or on nuclear reactors or hydraulics.

The fact of the matter is that everything you want to learn about absolutely anything can be found in books!

ABOUT THE AUTHOR

Harvey Weiss has written and illustrated many popular books for children, among them THE GADGET BOOK, HAMMER AND SAW: *An Introduction to Woodworking,* HOW TO BE AN INVENTOR, HOW TO MAKE YOUR OWN BOOKS, HOW TO RUN A RAILROAD: *Everything You Need to Know About Model Trains,* MODEL AIRPLANES AND HOW TO BUILD THEM, MODEL BUILDINGS AND HOW TO MAKE THEM, MODEL CARS AND TRUCKS AND HOW TO BUILD THEM, and MOTORS AND ENGINES AND HOW THEY WORK. A distinguished sculptor whose work has received many awards and has been exhibited in galleries and museums across the country, he brings to his books a sure sense of what appeals to and can be accomplished by young people, and a sculptor's eye for simple, uncluttered forms.

Mr. Weiss is professor of sculpture at Adelphi University and lives in Greens Farms, Connecticut.